Trust in the Lord with all your heart and lean not on your own understanding; in all your ways submit to him and he will make your paths straight

Proverbs 3:5-6

Printed by CreateSpace, An Amazon.com Company

Date: _____

My Requests:

Bible Verse:

My Prayer:

Answers:

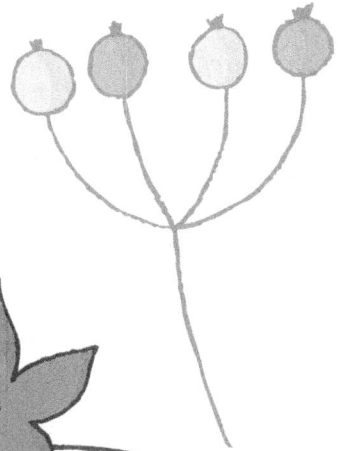

Thank You, Lord For...

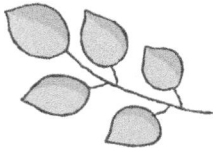

Date: _____

My Requests:

Bible Verse:

My Prayer:

Answers:

Thank You, Lord For...

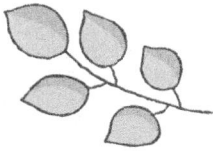

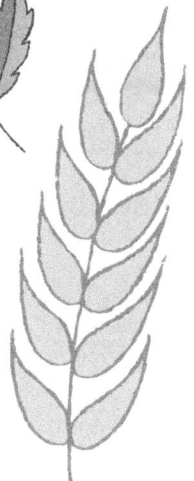

Date: _____

My Requests:

Bible Verse:

My Prayer:

Answers:

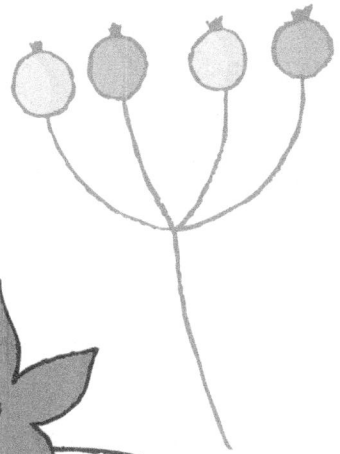

Thank You, Lord For...

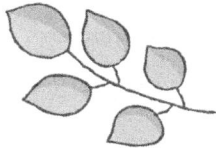

Date: _____

My Requests:

Bible Verse:

My Prayer:

Answers:

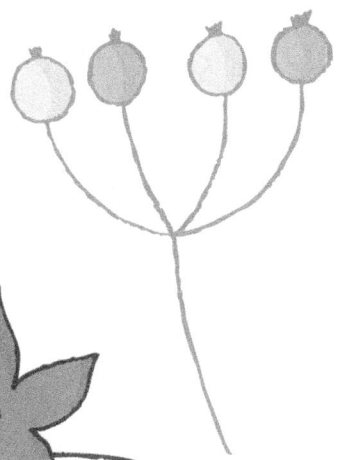

Thank You, Lord For...

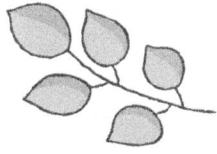

Date: _____

My Requests:

Bible Verse:

My Prayer:

Answers:

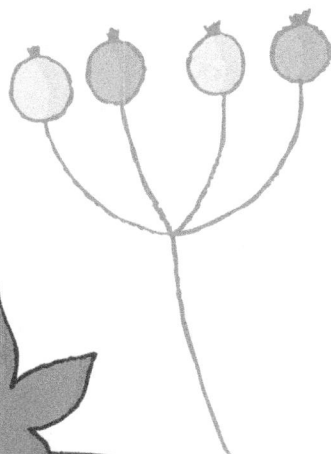

Thank You, Lord For...

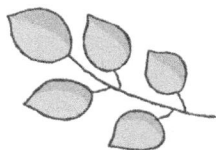

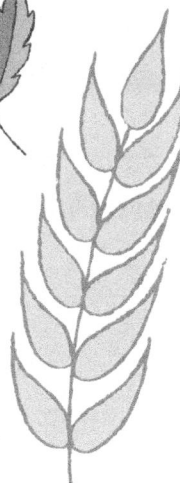

Date: _____

My Requests:

Bible Verse:

My Prayer:

Answers:

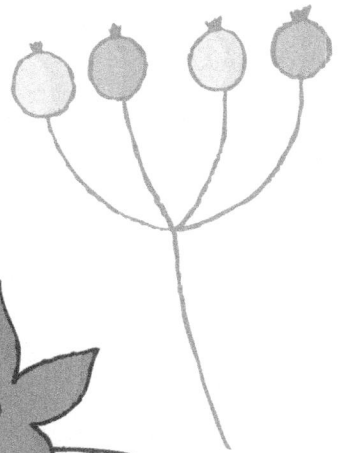

Thank You, Lord For...

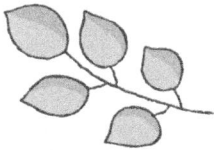

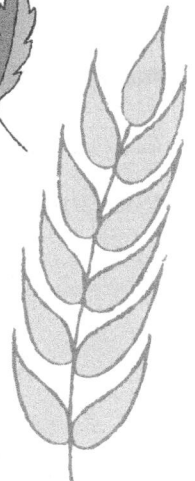

Date: _____

My Requests:

Bible Verse:

My Prayer:

Answers:

Thank You, Lord For...

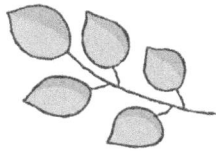

Date: _____

My Requests:

Bible Verse:

My Prayer:

Answers:

Thank You, Lord For...

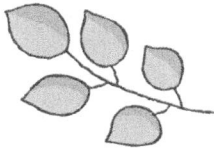

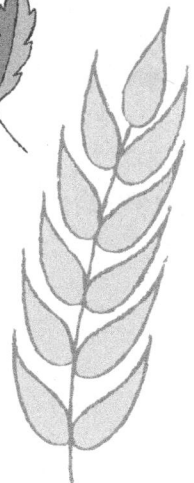

Date: _____

My Requests:

Bible Verse:

My Prayer:

Answers:

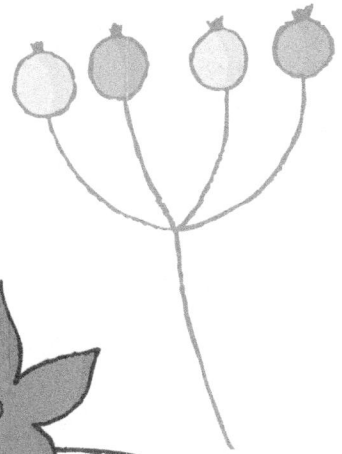

Thank You, Lord For...

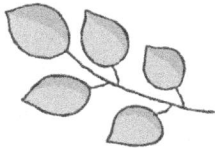

Date: _____

My Requests:

Bible Verse:

My Prayer:

Answers:

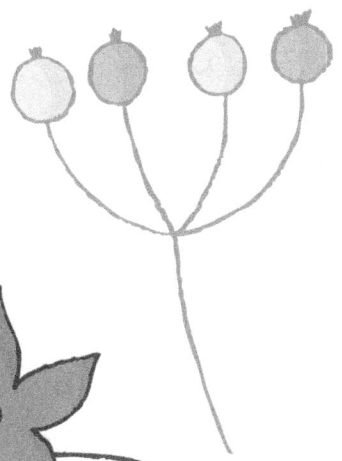

Thank You, Lord For...

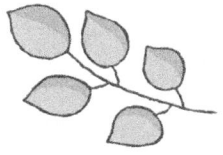

Date: _____

My Requests:

Bible Verse:

My Prayer:

Answers:

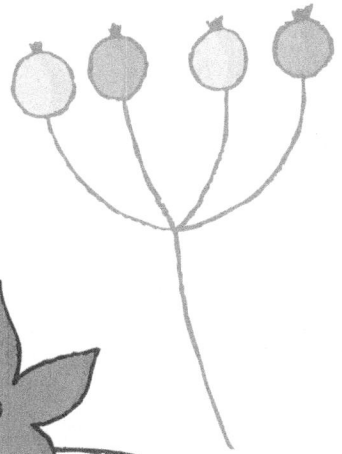

Thank You, Lord For...

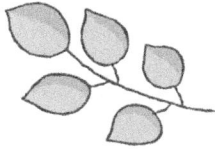

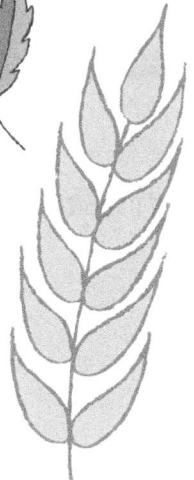

Date: _____

My Requests:

Bible Verse:

My Prayer:

Answers:

Thank You, Lord For...

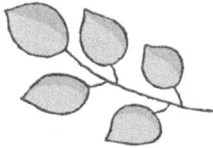

Date: _____

My Requests:

Bible Verse:

My Prayer:

Answers:

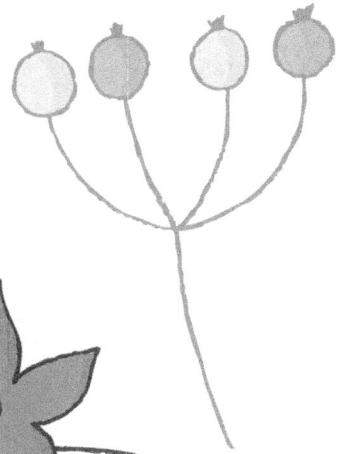

Thank You, Lord For...

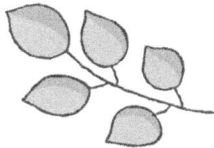

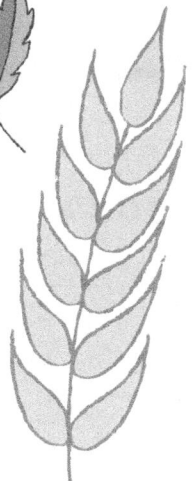

Date: _____

My Requests:

Bible Verse:

My Prayer:

Answers:

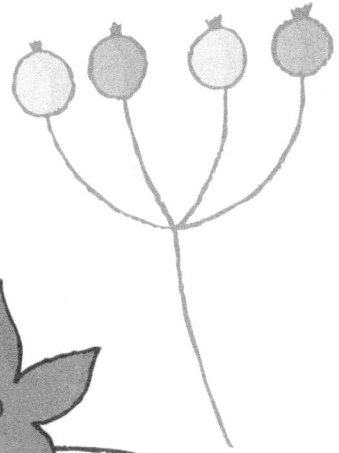

Thank You, Lord For...

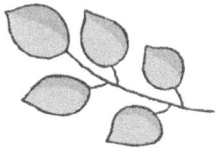

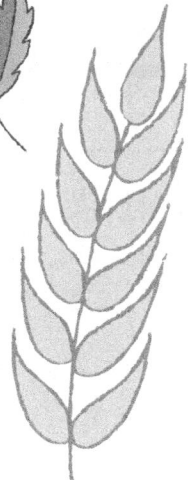

Date: _____

My Requests:

Bible Verse:

My Prayer:

Answers:

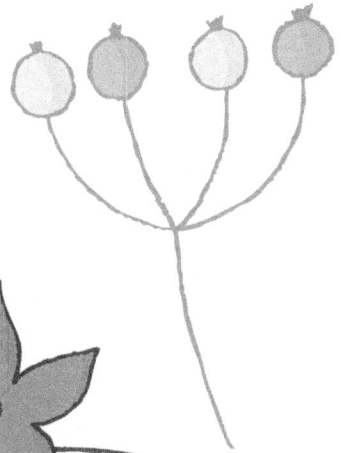

Thank You, Lord For...

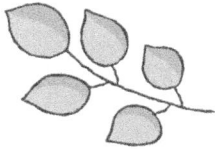

Date: _____

My Requests:

Bible Verse:

My Prayer:

Answers:

Thank You, Lord For...

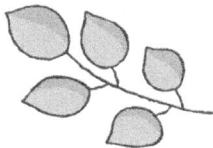

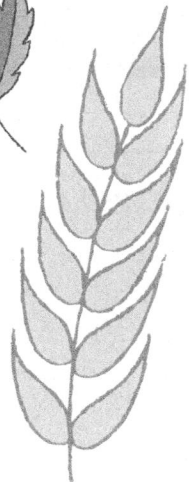

Date: _____

My Requests:

Bible Verse:

My Prayer:

Answers:

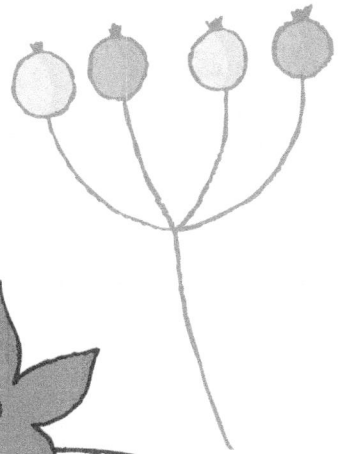

Thank You, Lord For...

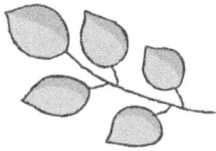

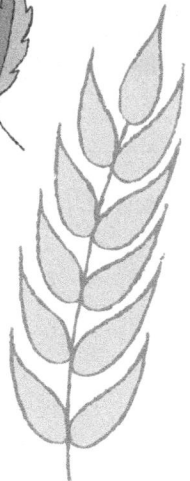

Date: _____

My Requests:

Bible Verse:

My Prayer:

Answers:

Thank You, Lord For...

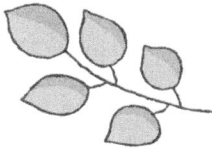

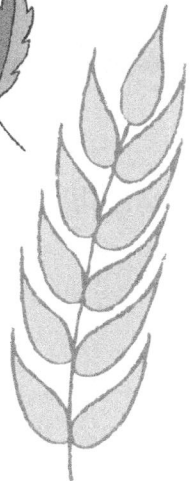

Date: _____

My Requests:

Bible Verse:

My Prayer:

Answers:

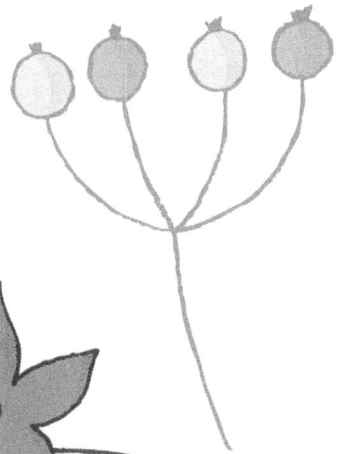

Thank You, Lord For...

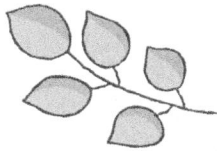

Date: _____

My Requests:

Bible Verse:

My Prayer:

Answers:

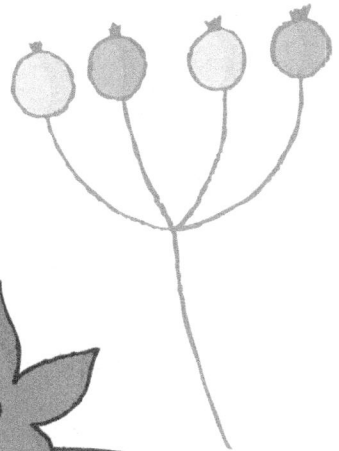

Thank You, Lord For...

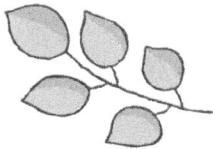

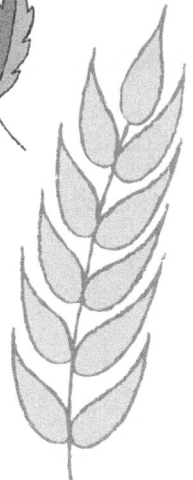

Date: _____

My Requests:

Bible Verse:

My Prayer:

Answers:

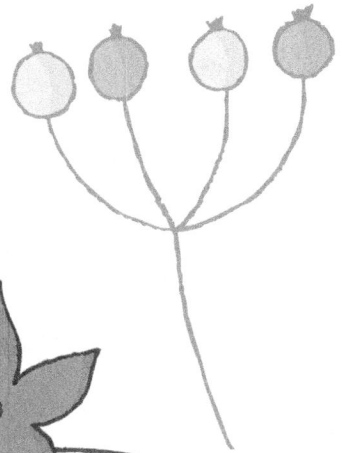

Thank You, Lord For...

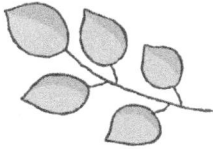

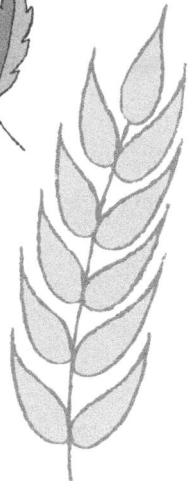

Date: _____

My Requests:

Bible Verse:

My Prayer:

Answers:

Thank You, Lord For...

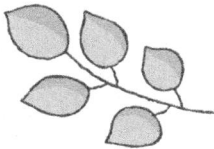

Date: _____

My Requests:

Bible Verse:

My Prayer:

Answers:

Thank You, Lord For...

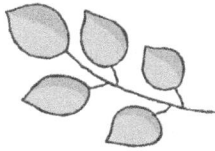

Date: _____

My Requests:

Bible Verse:

My Prayer:

Answers:

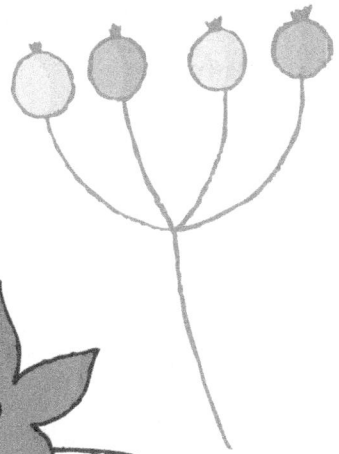

Thank You, Lord For...

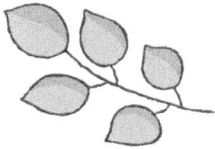

Date: _____

My Requests:

Bible Verse:

My Prayer:

Answers:

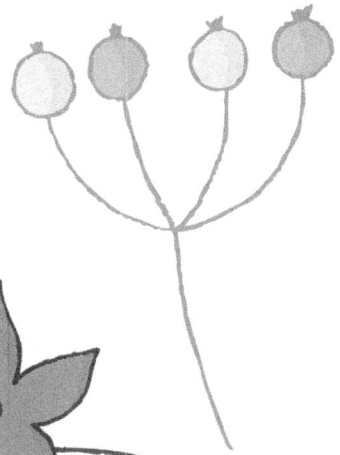

Thank You, Lord For...

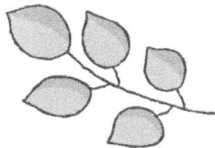

Date: _____

My Requests:

Bible Verse:

My Prayer:

Answers:

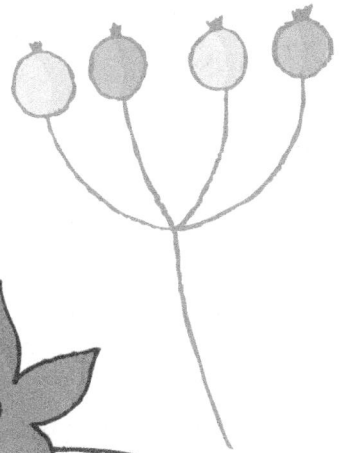

Thank You, Lord For...

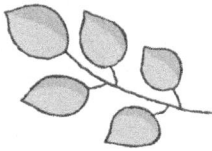

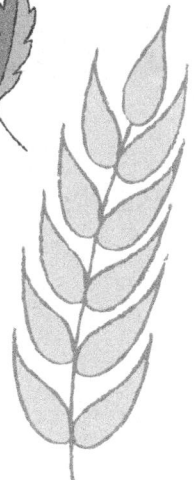

Date: _____

My Requests:

Bible Verse:

My Prayer:

Answers:

Thank You, Lord For...

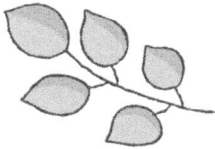

Date: _____

My Requests:

Bible Verse:

My Prayer:

Answers:

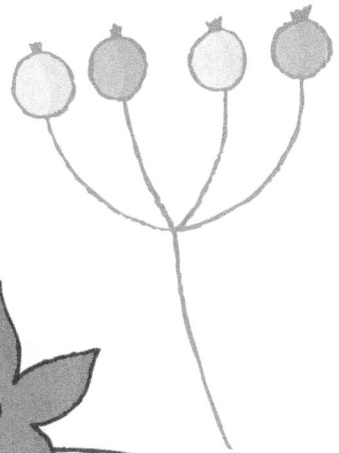

Thank You, Lord For...

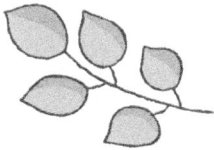

Date: _____

My Requests:

Bible Verse:

My Prayer:

Answers:

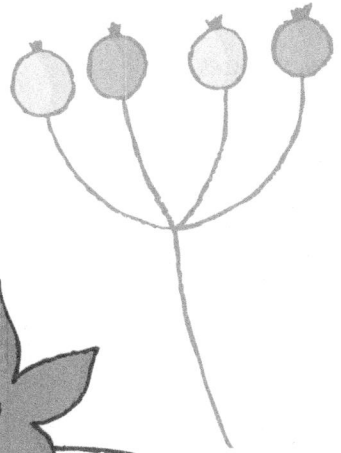

Thank You, Lord For...

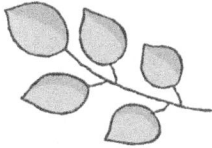

Date: _____

My Requests:

Bible Verse:

My Prayer:

Answers:

Thank You, Lord For...

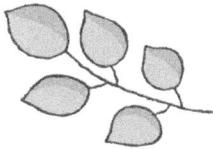

Date: _____

My Requests:

Bible Verse:

My Prayer:

Answers:

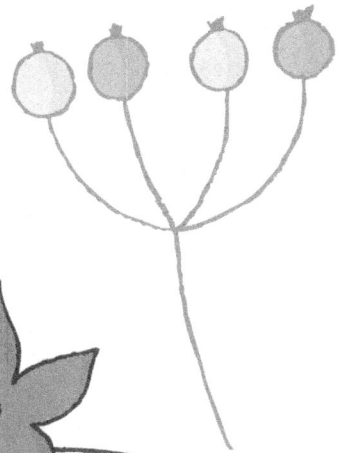

Thank You, Lord For...

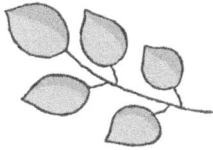

Date: _____

My Requests:

Bible Verse:

My Prayer:

Answers:

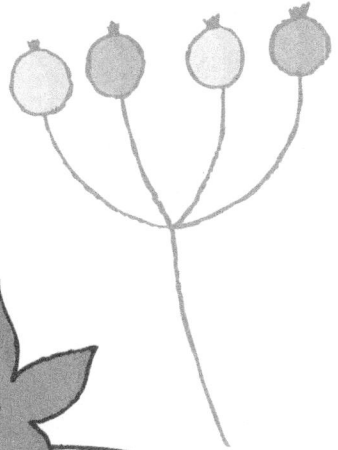

Thank You, Lord For...

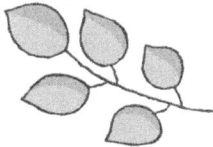

Date: _____

My Requests:

Bible Verse:

My Prayer:

Answers:

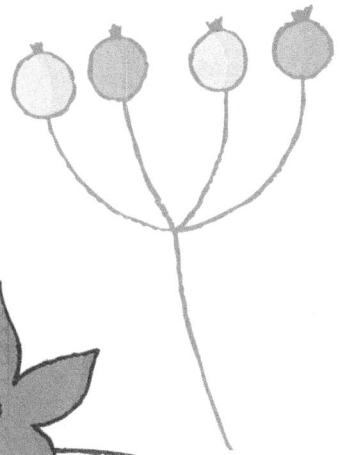

Thank You, Lord For...

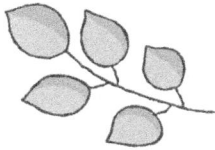

Date: _____

My Requests:

Bible Verse:

My Prayer:

Answers:

Thank You, Lord For...

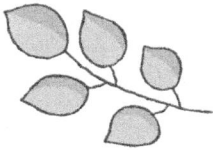

Date: _____

My Requests:

Bible Verse:

My Prayer:

Answers:

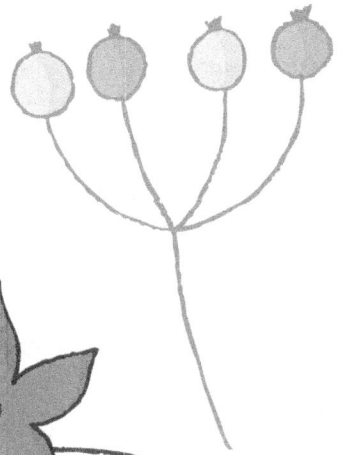

Thank You, Lord For...

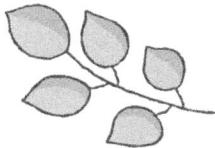

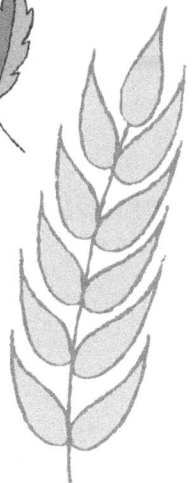

Date: _____

My Requests:

Bible Verse:

My Prayer:

Answers:

Thank You, Lord For...

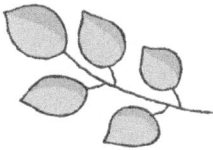

Date: _____

My Requests:

Bible Verse:

My Prayer:

Answers:

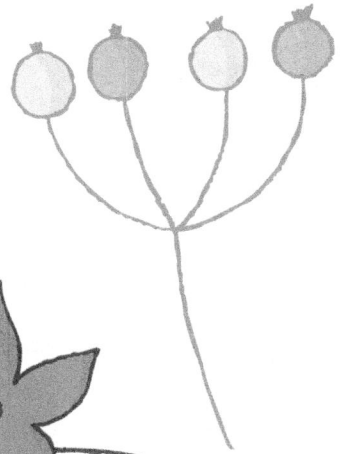

Thank You, Lord For...

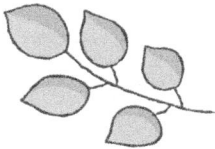

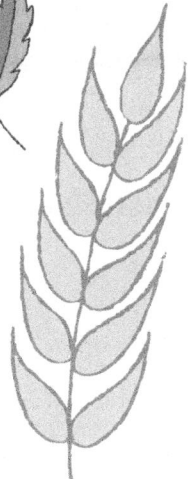

Date: _____

My Requests:

Bible Verse:

My Prayer:

Answers:

Thank You, Lord For...

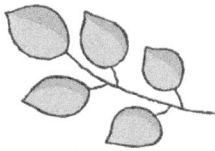

Date: _____

My Requests:

Bible Verse:

My Prayer:

Answers:

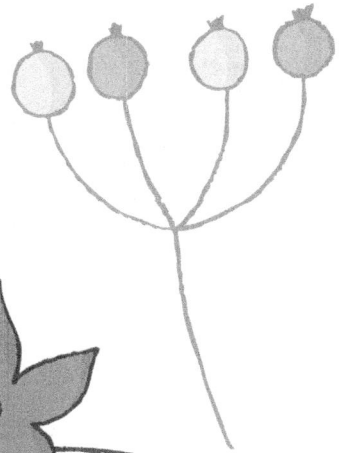

Thank You, Lord For...

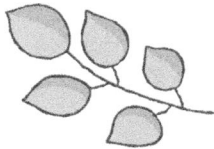

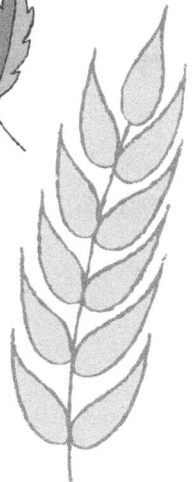

Date: _____

My Requests:

Bible Verse:

My Prayer:

Answers:

Thank You, Lord For...

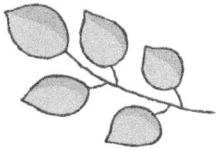

Date: _____

My Requests:

Bible Verse:

My Prayer:

Answers:

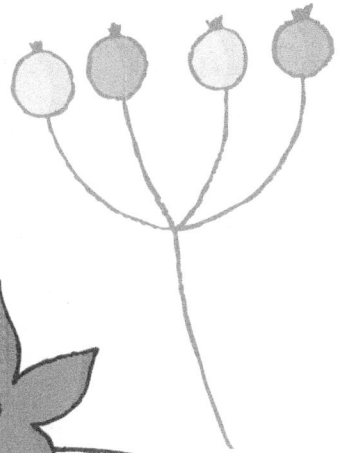

Thank You, Lord For...

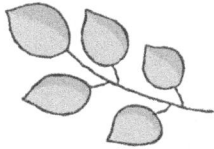

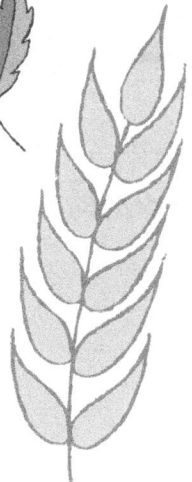

Date: _____

My Requests:

Bible Verse:

My Prayer:

Answers:

Thank You, Lord For...

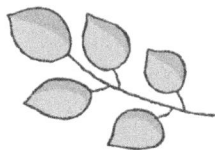

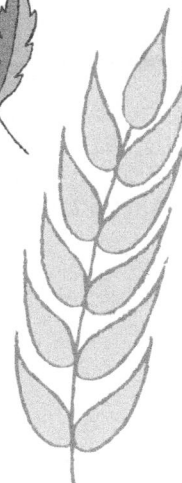

Date: _____

My Requests:

Bible Verse:

My Prayer:

Answers:

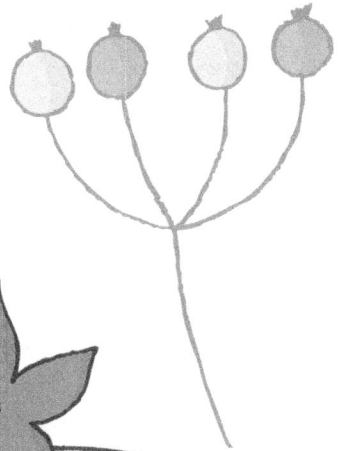

Thank You, Lord For...

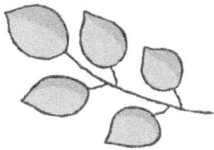

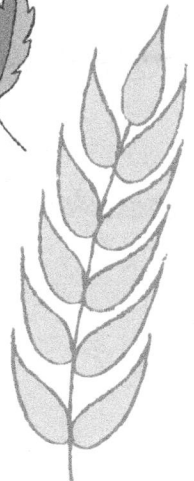

Date: _____

My Requests:

Bible Verse:

My Prayer:

Answers:

Thank You, Lord For...

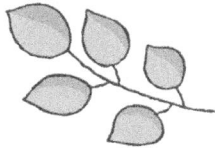

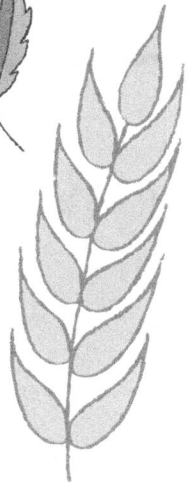

Date: _____

My Requests:

Bible Verse:

My Prayer:

Answers:

Thank You, Lord For...

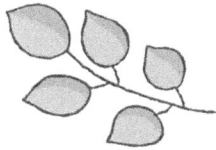

Date: _____

My Requests:

Bible Verse:

My Prayer:

Answers:

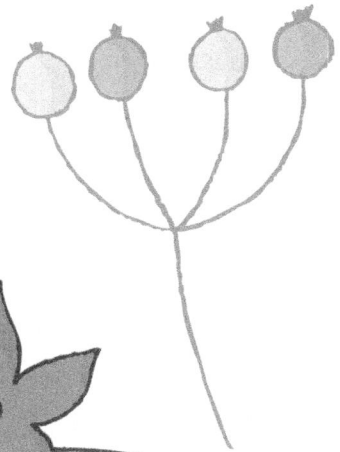

Thank You, Lord For...

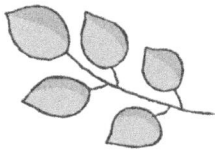

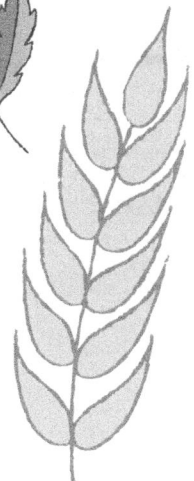

Date: _____

My Requests:

Bible Verse:

My Prayer:

Answers:

Thank You, Lord For...

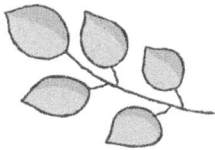

Date: _____

My Requests:

Bible Verse:

My Prayer:

Answers:

Thank You, Lord For...

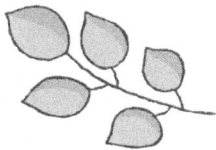

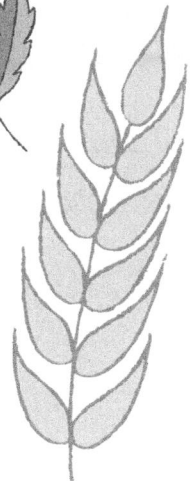

Date: _____

My Requests:

Bible Verse:

My Prayer:

Answers:

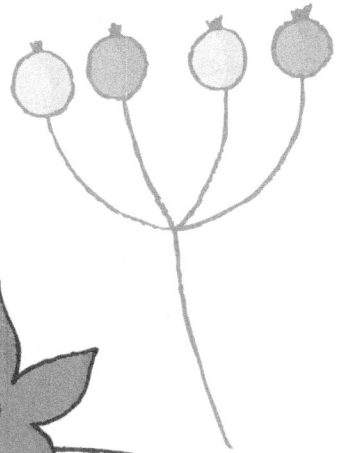

Thank You, Lord For...

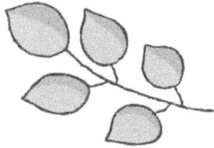

Date: _____

My Requests:

Bible Verse:

My Prayer:

Answers:

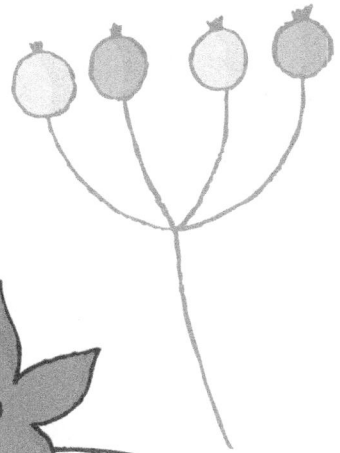

Thank You, Lord For...

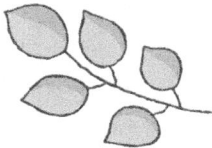

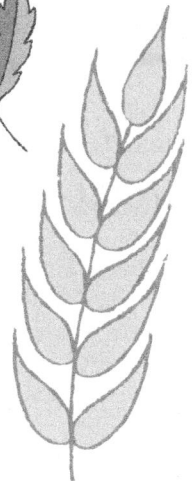

Date: _____

My Requests:

Bible Verse:

My Prayer:

Answers:

Thank You, Lord For...

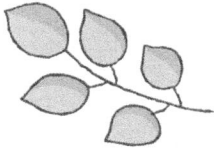

Date: _____

My Requests:

Bible Verse:

My Prayer:

Answers:

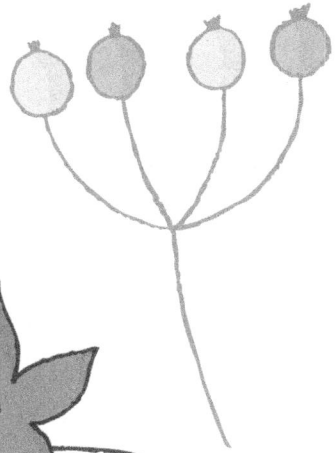

Thank You, Lord For...

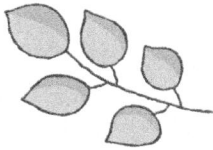

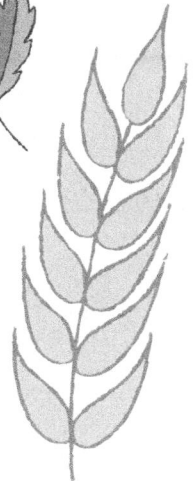

Date: _____

My Requests:

Bible Verse:

My Prayer:

Answers:

Thank You, Lord For...

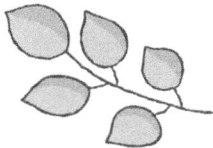

Date: _____

My Requests:

Bible Verse:

My Prayer:

Answers:

Thank You, Lord For...

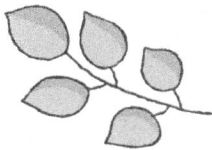

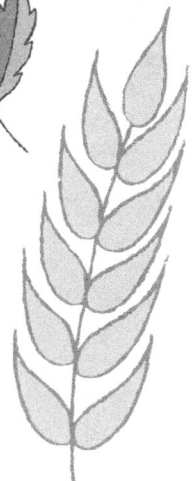

Date: _____

My Requests:

Bible Verse:

My Prayer:

Answers:

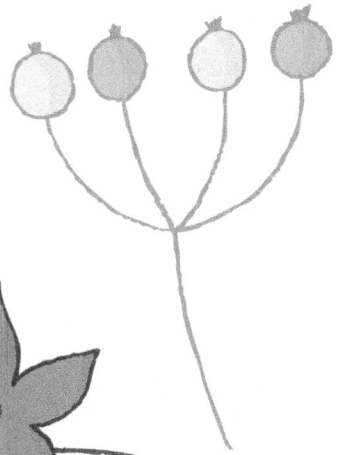

Thank You, Lord For...

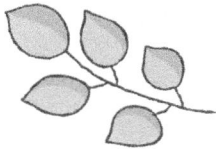

Date: _____

My Requests:

Bible Verse:

My Prayer:

Answers:

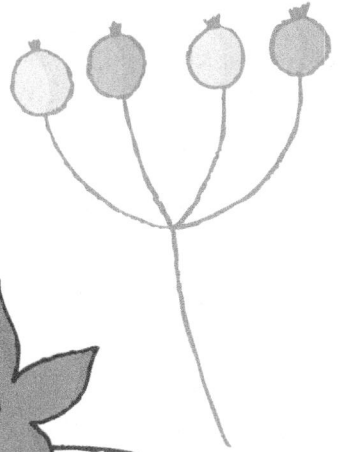

Thank You, Lord For...

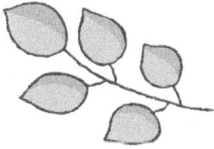

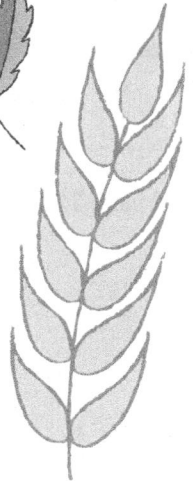

Date: _____

My Requests:

Bible Verse:

My Prayer:

Answers:

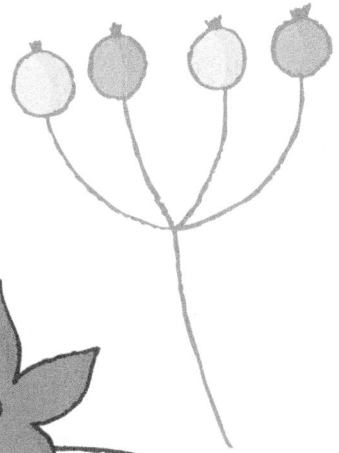

Thank You, Lord For...

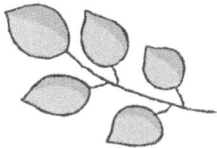

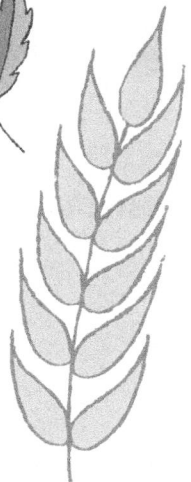

Date: _____

My Requests:

Bible Verse:

My Prayer:

Answers:

Thank You, Lord For...

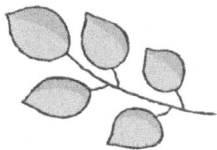

Date: _____

My Requests:

Bible Verse:

My Prayer:

Answers:

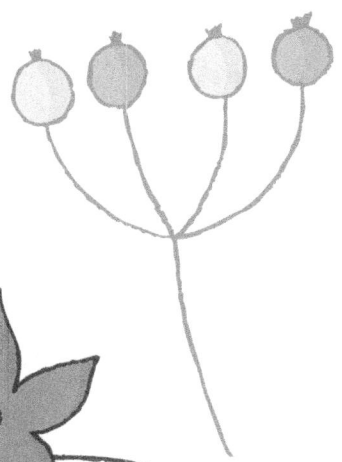

Thank You, Lord For...

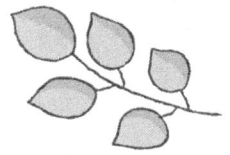

Date: _____

My Requests:

Bible Verse:

My Prayer:

Answers:

Thank You, Lord For...

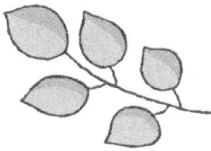

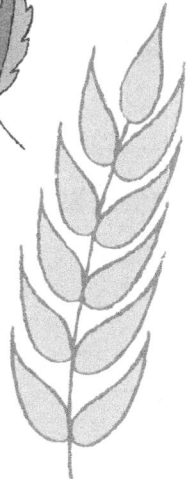

Date: _____

My Requests:

Bible Verse:

My Prayer:

Answers:

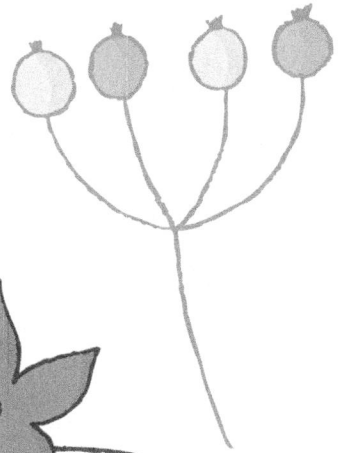

Thank You, Lord For...

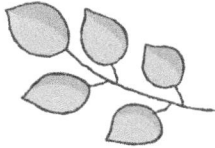

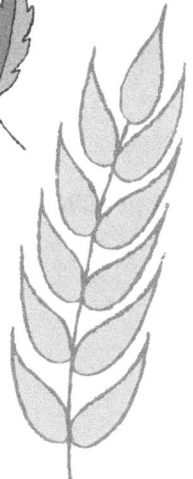

Date: _____

My Requests:

Bible Verse:

My Prayer:

Answers:

Thank You, Lord For...

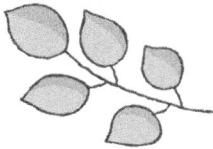

Date: _____

My Requests:

Bible Verse:

My Prayer:

Answers:

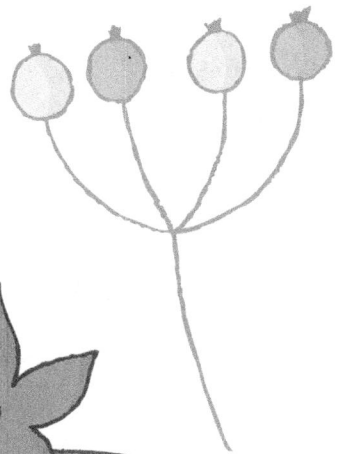

Thank You, Lord For...

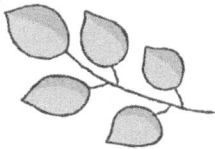

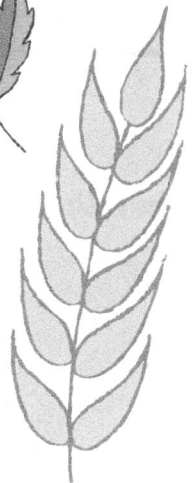

Date: _____

My Requests:

Bible Verse:

My Prayer:

Answers:

Thank You, Lord For...

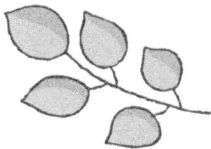

Date: _____

My Requests:

Bible Verse:

My Prayer:

Answers:

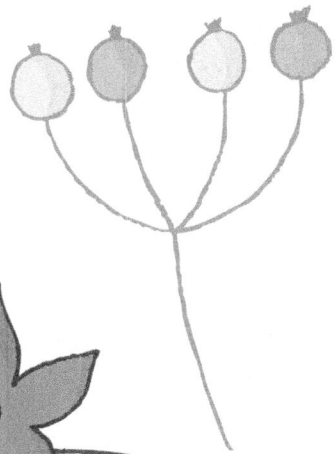

Thank You, Lord For...

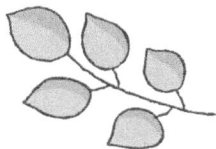

Date: _____

My Requests:

Bible Verse:

My Prayer:

Answers:

Thank You, Lord For...

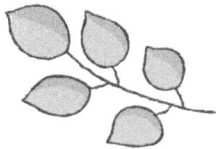

Made in the USA
Las Vegas, NV
14 December 2021